BETH MARTIN SYPHERS

is a flower farmer, wedding coordinator, and florist who resides in Rickreall, Oregon, in an idyllic historic farmhouse surrounded by roses, peonies, sweet peas, and dahlias. Along with her husband Jayson, daughter Rilley and son Brayden and an assortment of barnyard animals, they operate Crowley House Flower Farm & Studio. Creative and driven, she is a constant blur of energy and a bubbling source of enthusiasm.

SARAH MARTIN KUENZI

says she is still trying to decide what she wants to be when she grows up. She is a lover of plants, people, the compiling of words, and basically anything that is a challenge (as long as that demand does not require a long attention span). Sarah is a proud mama of two amazing boys, and is enjoying the new addition of a daughter-in-law. She is wife to Farmer K, a grass-seed farmer. She's happiest when puttering in her garden, creating concoctions in her kitchen, or throwing an impromptu dinner party. She lives in Silverton, Oregon, just a few miles from the Martin childhood home.

EMMA MAY DIXON

is an Oregon-based flower farmer and designer who has a love for photography. Through her lens, Emma captures the visual language of the garden, the home, and everyday moments of life as it unfolds. These are the moments she chases as she works with her family and helps tell their stories. Emma explains, "There are many moments that people are too busy to notice, especially in nature, but those are the moments for which I feel grateful, especially if I am the only observer."

furrow & flour

Publisher: **BLOOM Imprint**

Authors: **SARAH KUENZI + BETH SYPHERS**

Photographer: **EMMA MAY DIXON**

Editorial Director: **DEBRA PRINZING**

Creative Director: **ROBIN AVNI**

Copy Editor: **PAULA PANICH**

Cover Designer + Image Editor: **JENNY M. DIAZ**

Photo Stylist: **RILLEY SYPHERS**

ISBN: 978-1736848173

Library of Congress Control Number: 2023931338

BLOOM Imprint
4810 Pt. Fosdick Drive NW, #297, Gig Harbor, WA 98335
www.bloomimprint.com

Printed in the U.S.A. by Consolidated Press, Seattle, WA

furrow & flour

Family stories, life lessons, and inspiration
from the garden and for the home

BETH SYPHERS & SARAH KUENZI

PHOTOGRAPHY BY EMMA MAY DIXON

welcome

Come in and make yourself comfortable.

These words, in whatever language, are known the world over. They offer a drink to the thirsty, food for the hungry, a place for shelter from the rain; along with safety, peace, inspiration, conversation, and friendship.

We four sisters were born in the space of five years and grew up as the eldest of twelve Martin siblings in a country house on a hill overlooking the Willamette Valley in Oregon. Our lives were shaped by the four seasons, which is also how the narrative of Furrow & Flour unfolds.

We were blessed to grow up in a home that provided welcome to those who crossed its threshold. No matter the circumstances, no matter the season, this warmth and virtual embrace were evident to all. We didn't have a fancy, perfect life, but what we did receive has been a gift carried with us into adulthood. Sisters numbers two and three, Beth Martin Syphers and Sarah Martin Kuenzi, will share a bit of the best with you, dear reader.

FALL. I'm Amber, and as the eldest, I usually was the bossy one who made sure tasks were completed and that everything looked beautiful. By aesthetically pleasing I don't mean perfect — just cozy, comfortable, and serviceably clean. None of us are perfectionists … we are realists who know that at the end of the day, friends and family remember the good food, lively conversation, and a thought-provoking connection with others, as opposed to a spotless house, gourmet meal, and a seamlessly curated evening. Now, in my home in Canada, I often think back to life lessons from childhood. I have learned to let go, just relax, and offer the gift of hospitality to my family, friends, and visitors to our flower farm and studio.

SUMMER. Sarah has always been the most flamboyant one in our family. She's a hostess with pizzazz, heart, an amazing sense of effortless style, and always has a witty remark that will make you snort with laughter. She has summer sizzle and a knack for seeing thoughtful and quirky details, often catching her observations in watercolor or sketches that add detail to family celebrations. She's also the best in the kitchen, hands down.

SPRING. Beth, the big-hearted owner of Crowley House Flower Farm, is the steady glue that holds us all together. She is the cheerful one to offer encouragement and is a mentor to many. She is the one who gets things done! Her lovely flower farm is an inspiring place filled with the beauty of nature and a kind welcome.

WINTER. Our sister Mary is the life of the party, a mile a minute conversationalist and a radiating warmth. This sister has been tested by the winter storms of life and still holds onto what really matters. Time spent inside her farmhouse remains long after you have left its shelter. Mary's daughter Emma May Dixon, whose images illustrate this book and who farms with Beth and her family, is a creative force in her own right.

The greatest gift our parents have given to us is awareness; the ability to see others, take in our surroundings, and sense the needs of those who come into our circle. It was taught not only in words, but mainly by example. Each one of us has felt the benefits of this knowledge as life has led us down diverse pathways and highways spanning this country and beyond.

This book is a taste of 'home' that we wish to share with you. So welcome to a snapshot of our lives, co-created by my sisters Sarah and Beth, with input from the entire Martin gang and beautifully captured in images by our niece Emma, Mary's daughter, with styling assistance by Rilley Syphers, Beth's daughter. All of the recipes are family-tested in our kitchens here, in Canada, and from Oregon to Hawaii, by willing siblings, in-laws, and budding, third-generation foodies.

Kick off your shoes, curl up and get cozy while I pour the coffee. We are all friends and you are welcome here.

AMBER TIEDE

SISTER NUMBER ONE
ONTARIO, CANADA

two of twelve

There are so many lives we and our sisters have wished to live, so many adventures just out of reach, so many words left unspoken. Sometimes it is easy to be bogged down with all the perceived missteps that have led us down dusty dirt roads rather than traipsing through France or scaling a corporate ladder.

Yet if we are honest with ourselves, we're not those girls.

We are content talking to hens while throwing scratch. We find an unreasonable amount of joy from cooking in kitchens close to our hearts, and actually enjoy swiping at dust and straightening pictures. A perfect evening ends not bedecked and bedazzled but curled on a cushion — either outside with the crickets, or in the corner of the couch with a glass of wine and a fabulous book.

What has charted our course to where we are now begins with a tangle of childhood memories. We are two of twelve children, eight sisters and four brothers born between 1969 and 1989. We grew up in a five-bedroom house on the outskirts of Keizer, Oregon, with a big garden and plenty of room to play.

Beth and Sarah are the sandwich girls in the top of a triple-decker Dagwood concoction; the two in the middle of the four that made up "the big girls," as our mother and father called us.

the 12 martin siblings

Our parents found pure joy in the simple life they created and even though it wasn't always perfect, it was a life formed out of love, and at the heart of it all were we twelve children.

the big girls

ONE
AMBER b. 1969

TWO
SARAH b. 1971

THREE
BETH b. 1972

FOUR
MARY b. 1974

the little kids

FIVE
STUART b. 1976

SIX
RACHEL b. 1978

SEVEN
CAROL b. 1979

EIGHT
VIRGINIA b. 1981

the babies

NINE
JONATHAN b. 1983

TEN
KEITH b. 1985

ELEVEN
ARWEN b. 1987

TWELVE
ELEANOR b. 1989

We were followed by the next third, named "the little kids," and they were followed by "the babies" — two boys and two girls that were our family's youngest. We learned from an early age to change diapers, bus tables, and weed a vegetable row. While friends slept in on a Saturday, we would rise and shine, or grumble and complain — depending on the day or how bright the memory. Perusing the large whiteboard in the laundry room, our fingers followed the row of chores that were ours for the week, and then we got to them.

We can still see the triangle of sunlight that finds its way to the threadbare Persian rug as dad kisses mom goodbye in the doorway before work.

Suddenly, we kids are paddling madly in our boat made of light down the Amazon River in the jungle of our overactive imaginations. It's almost as if we can smell the pungent scent of the earth after a soaking rain and see the delicate fairy cap of a pristine lily-of-the-valley glowing under the dense cover of lush vegetation.

Our mouths watered as we waited for that slice of sun-warmed tomato, all saucy and sloppy on a bed of sprouts and a mass of cream cheese slathered across a thick slice of whole wheat or sourdough bread. It's a gaggle of girls, seven of us, lanky and tanned, keeping tabs on the young ones that are making mud pies and scrabbling in the shallows.

It's the breeze through open windows carrying our voices as we try out new melodies to wrap up the day. There was always music from the cassette player; Strauss, Beethoven, and Mozart to promote that extra twirl as we dusted or vacuumed. We'd set the long dining room table with its assortment of hodgepodge chairs and the piano bench for extra seating and everyday china acquired from saved Green Stamps, adding a mix of glass goblets and Tupperware cups and a oddball collection of silverware, all the while wearing our roller skates, making it possible to swing wildly around each corner and practice our backwards sashay.

Outdoors was a kaleidoscope of color: layers of texture and the rowdy mix of edible, and ornamental blooms.

We'd shrink down in our bus seats in early spring as the rest of the children squealed and held their noses at the smell of freshly delivered cow manure, knowing full well who the culprits were. Sure enough, after rounding the house, there was Pop, joyously turning under this newly acquired fertilizer into his vegetable patch.

Our house had a revolving door. We hosted newlyweds for Christmas with a rousing rendition of "bring me a figgy pudding," which in real life had ignited into a four-alarm blaze (no, more rum-soaked sugar cubes are not necessarily better)! We had neighborhood kids clambering over fences, taffy pulls and harvest parties with apple bobbing, and popcorn balls studded with candy-corn. Folding chairs were pulled from closets and main dishes scooped a bit less generously so all could partake.

With the lively and warm conversation that flowed around the table, it never even occurred to us that mom had been paddling madly under the surface to make it all come together.

Being raised in a home without a television was an embarrassment. As a kids, we cringed when the classroom conversation swung to Obi-Wan Kenobi, or *Mork and Mindy.*

While desperately lacking knowledge of pop culture, our minds were filled with Dad's deep, theatrical voice; we knew of the elfin kingdoms of Rivendell, the oppressive rank of Mordor, and followed the iridescent glow from Gandalf's staff as he led us through the dales and up the rocky sides of mountains, long before New Line Cinema made Lord of the Rings a household name.

Along with the shelves of paperbacks that made up our library was a prized possession: a dollhouse that we dearly loved and spent countless hours decorating. We would make up stories with all the kiddos gathered round on the shag of the bedroom floor, conducting our own version of cartoon plots. No childhood is completely devoid of dark times and drama, although we were fortunate to live in a bubble of security, there on 13th Avenue.

Mornings brought stories read while mom pulled a brush though the long lines of heads that would be tamed with braids by the time Almanzo had the pigs slopped or Laura had washed her tin cup and was under quilts in the wagon.

We took our lazy naps (or quiet times) in which we swapped secrets or snuck up to the roof lugging our Caboodle stuffed with tinfoil, baby oil and a self-made tape of Casey Cason's top 40 hits along with a pink boom box to work on our one sided-tans, soaking up the rays till Mom got wise and called us down.

There were Sunday drives in the rolling hills outside of Silverton, the maxi van stuffed to the brim with bodies and smelling of PB&J's, and rode our bikes beneath the thick canopy of the gnarled hazelnut orchard with the boys from next door.

All of us girls shared a room under the dormers and almost every night we sang ourselves to sleep,

> Oh, meet me when daylight is fading,
>   and darkening into the night,
> When songbirds are singing their vespers
> And the day has vanished from sight
> And then I will tell you, my darling
> Of the love I have cherished so long
> If you will but meet me this evening
> When you hear the first whippoorwill's song.

BETH & SARAH

SPRING

SUMMER

AUTUMN

WINTER

SPRING

spring has sprung!

This season compels us to burst forth with vim and vigor, conquering the dust-bunnies lurking under couch cushions and cobwebs that have hidden in plain sight, but went unobserved by candlelight and winter's gloom. Let's shake out the rugs and switch the bedding from flannel to cotton sheets! Away with the muted tone throw pillows and in with the vibrant hues. Fill all available jugs and jam jars with bobbing daffodils, branches of soft-petal cherry blossom, yellow forsythia, and fragrant clusters of blushing daphne; adorning all shiny clean surfaces with blousy blooms that seem to glow in the watery afternoon sunlight.

It is the season of new birth and young love, all gangly and awkward as it moves on unsteady feet with feelings etched on sleeves — both in the animal kingdom and in the high school halls. Young lambs bounce and collide with enthusiasm and adolescent steers play "leap-frog" in the pasture (look away, children!). Gawky teens are hovering a beat longer at the locker door, hoping for a perfectly timed encounter on their way to sixth period. Remember that heart-pounding moment when eyes would meet, and elbows brushed?

Spring mimics a flute concerto as it dips, flutters, and flies. It is captured in the freshness of linens snapping on a clothesline as a flirtatious breeze dances in and about its edges. Spring lifts our hearts, warms our skin, creating a tingling of anticipation for renewal and adventure, both in the home and the open road that beckons just beyond the property line.

SARAH

a day in the life

The sun is just peeking over the hills to wake the farm. A light fog lays over the fields like a patchwork quilt in tints of pink and gold, flooding my world with romantic thoughts. It's the kind of morning you want to capture in your mind's eye, to hold onto in dark winter months.

Standing on the back steps and looking out over the gardens, I think to myself that Jane Austen's Mr. Darcy might stroll out of that magical mist. I'm rudely roused from my fantasy by the ducks yelling for their release as a splash in the pond is paramount, the chickens cluck-clucking as they line up by the gate, waiting on scratch, and the other farm creatures join in the clamoring for attention and breakfast. The morning air is fresh with the smell of spring, transported via a marriage of scents: newly-cut grass, blooming sweet peas, and lilac, along with the cooking smells of frying bacon and over-easy eggs.

There's the cheerful chatter and clatter as plates are stacked on the butcher-block counter, and coffee is poured into waiting mismatched mugs. Our daughter is giving a rambunctious account of last night's happenings and our son scoots in to grab a slice of buttered toast before dashing off to catch his ride to school, screen door slapping behind him. Weaving in and out of this comforting commotion is Shay (the farm dog), her tail

beating an enthusiastic rhythm, as she is impossibly ecstatic to see us. One could be led to believe it was days, rather than hours, since we last had been together.

The screen door squeaks behind me and is accompanied by a low wolf-whistle. "Looking gooood, dahlin'," Jason purrs, lowering himself to the porch step, clunky boots in hand. I tell him what I have on the go; he fills me in on the fields where he plans to spread fertilizer and mentions that the cows will need moving from the canyon, up to the pond pasture. With a coffee-scented kiss on the cheek, he says he'll do the chores before heading out and I tell him he's my hero. Underneath the flirtatious eye batting, I am serious.

> I make my way down the garden path,
> mug of tea in hand, visiting my favorite flowers;
> stopping to smell the newly blooming roses.

I can't help but feel my mounting enthusiasm for the upcoming season and the sight of little buds ready to explode. On the agenda today are a few orders to fill and a wedding to cut for. I remind myself to cut some for the house. The gardens are full of color, and there is so much to choose from. I take my clippers, fill a few clean buckets with fresh, cool water, and head out into

the flower fields. The tulips I planted last fall have pushed up in a breathtaking display and it almost feels a shame to cut them. I move on to peonies, sweet peas, ranunculus, and the first garden roses.

I think of the time I lived in a neighborhood of new homes all in a row with perfectly manicured lawns and repetitive landscape plantings from the big box garden centers. How I had yearned for the wild of a farm and the exhaustion (but exaltation) that life would bring.

I lived out my dreams through local magazines; where I read a beautiful story of an experienced lady who designed flowers with a lush, untamed style as she incorporated the ramblings of nature in all its vivacious stages. It was all so different from what I observed around me.

> I asked if I might visit. She replied,
> "Yes, please come visit. Come for tea."

Driving to Portland with butterflies in my stomach, I was grateful for the hour of grownup music and the opportunity for my thoughts to wander uninterrupted. Arriving, I took in the house clothed in brilliant color, the plants diverse in texture, and blooms unknown to me. There was a long brick path lined with mossy stones and scattered with violets, leading to an aged apple-green garden gate.

Her warm voice greeted me as I made my way into the backyard with her shaggy dog as my escort. In the small woodland setting behind her home, she had created a world of immense beauty. With a smile and her obvious *joie de vivre*, this generous stranger offered me the affirmation and confidence to pursue a life with my garden at the center.

She poured tea; our conversation flowed as if we were old friends. At the end of the day, I left that magical space filled with a wealth of information and creative inspiration. I knew I would never be the same again.

With that memory, I gather up the buckets of blooms and head back to the studio. As my hands set to work arranging, I feel a wave of gratitude for the people who took time to instruct me, cared enough to encourage and listen, and then to gently push me on. I think of my eldest sister, her patience while teaching me floral design, as I was just a teen and eager to learn but had no clue and limited attention span. I remember my father answering all my many questions on how to grow plants.

My grandmothers created beautiful gardens, ranging from small raised beds or a collection of pots, to an expansive tropical oasis that to this day still inspires me.

I think of the books I've read by the many horticultural writers and floral designers who have paved the way, making my pursuit of a flower-filled life that much easier with their wisdom and knowledge.

I finish up a grand display of fragrant blooms for the upcoming wedding, tucking the last leftover snippets into vintage bud vases to scatter around our home. My heart is thankful for the opportunity and encouragement to fulfill the dreams that had existed in my head. They now feed my soul.

BETH

slow work of art

When you find it hard to cut your blooms from your garden because they look so beautiful as they are, it's time to give yourself a dedicated cutting garden. Here are some ideas for designing and planting a flower-filled garden:

ONE. Pick a sunny spot and choose a style of garden to fit the available space, whether it be a collection of pots, several raised beds, or an established planting area.

TWO. Select plants that look good in vase displays, including a mix for all seasons. Plant flowering bulbs in fall or early spring. I like to plant in raised beds as well as in a few terracotta pots. I keep them in my greenhouse until the weather warms, giving them a few weeks' advantage to endure late frost. From tulips, daffodils, grape hyacinths, snowdrops, and anemones, the spring-flowering bulb list is always exciting. Consider planting 'cool flowers' in fall to winter over, or sow seeds in early spring: Bachelor's button, snapdragons, and stock.

THREE. After the spring show begins to die back, keep planting annuals like cosmos, zinnias, and sunflowers. Planting a mix will allow for more bloom variety. This is a garden that you treat as your own special space, your source for cutting blooms for your house and to share with your friends.

BETH

a thousand first kisses

The breeze is balmy and fresh, carrying soft whispers of lilac blooms and the tang of recently mowed grass. My boy and I are kneeling on the still-chilly ground, fingers damp even through garden gloves. While popping out seedlings into an even row, he fills me in on the details of a girl, just newly discovered, who sits two desks away. She has big blue eyes and Heidi-from-the-mountains braids. She is funny and smart and runs faster than any of the boys and (I break in), related to us.

We have had this conversation before. When one's Dad comes from a huge farm family, and your grandparents grew up in an even larger clan, mixed with the fact that we live a mile and a half from where his father was raised … chances are great that most of your classmates in the small country school are distant relatives.

His little shoulders slump as he laments that he will never find anybody … EVER!

I assure him that the world is big; much larger than this one-stoplight town. Someday he will see. And besides, I add, your first kiss is special, there's only one of them in you, so there is absolutely no need to be in a rush to spend it. He ponders this for a minute, then settles back on his heels with a grin on his young face. "Mom, I can feel a thousand first kisses in me," he replies. I try to hide my smile.

I am cleaning tender spring greens at the kitchen sink when I see them. My nephew had sent a text wondering if it was okay to bring his new girl over for a picnic, to which I immediately tapped back an enthusiastic "Yes!!"

They are giddy and coltish; bumping shoulders, brushing hands, laughing a bit too loud, high on life and love and each other as they meander towards the old oak tree.

Out of nowhere, the sky clouds over and a rain shower falls. With a whoop, they run pell-mell towards the barn. They squeeze through the half-opened door and find shelter in the hay-scented alleyway of the structure.

This barn was built in the early 1900s; being a haven for young love is nothing new. I remember the almost-reverent feeling of looking high into its peak as the dust motes floated in a sunbeam — weightless, effortless, as if time and gravity were irrelevant.

In the barn sound is muffled, as if nothing else existed; the air is pungent with the scent of meadows and cow manure, baling twine, and oats. Through the open bat-winged doors, the gentle spring wind whisks in the notes of bird song, sending it drifting to land on young ears.

Evening sneaks up quietly, softening the edges of the day and turning the vibrant green to grey. We finish up the day's outdoor chores by feeding the fire pit's flames with branches and twigs torn from trees in winter's fury. The burning tinder sends a spiral of snapping sparks into the night sky.

Work done, we stand close to the heat, cold hands wrapped around stemless glasses of Merlot, breathing in the smell of mesquite-rubbed steak and roasting onion rounds, a chorus of baby frogs serenading us from the pond below. Life feels reborn, renewed, reclaimed.

We balance plates loaded with baby greens tossed with lemon vinaigrette, oven-roasted red potatoes sprinkled with dill, and steak alongside a caramel-colored onion. We prop our cold, boot-clad toes towards the flames, grateful for warmth.

Later, I tidy the kitchen and scrape the leftovers into storage containers as Farmer K is tucking the wee ones into bed. I hear them begging for "just one more story." It's a tossup between *Where the Wild Things Are* and *Jack and Annie and the Magic Tree House*. I find myself hoping the children hold these evenings in their memories, and when life is cold and uncertain, they may well offer a comforting place to return to.

SARAH

lemon herb vinaigrette

SERVES: 10

Bright and flavorful on any mix of greens from your garden patch or from a farmer's stand.

PREP TIME: 8-10 minutes

INGREDIENTS

1 tablespoon chives, snipped

1 garlic clove, minced

1 tablespoon fresh parsley, minced

1 tablespoon shallot, minced

1 teaspoon fresh thyme, minced

1 tablespoon honey

2 teaspoons Dijon mustard

3 tablespoons lemon juice, freshly squeezed (approximately one lemon)

½ cup extra virgin olive oil

¼ cup water

INSTRUCTIONS

Combine all ingredients in a medium bowl and whisk vigorously in order to emulsify. Refrigerate until needed.

cowboy steak rub

SERVES: 1 ½ cups for 2-4 servings

There was a time, years ago, when this girl held up her Wrangler jeans with a belt with a Black Hills gold buckle and her name stamped on the back. While marrying a cowboy and roaming the range was her dream, her heart was won by a handsome farmer with a horse on the side, and the ability to grill one impressive steak.

PREP TIME: 10 minutes

COOK TIME: 10 minutes

INGREDIENTS

I ½ cup chili powder

¼ cup ground coffee

¼ cup smoked paprika

¼ cup cumin

¼ cup brown sugar

2 teaspoons sea salt

2 teaspoons garlic powder

1 teaspoon onion powder

2 teaspoons dry mustard

2 teaspoons ground coriander

2 teaspoons fresh ground black pepper

1 teaspoon cayenne pepper

INSTRUCTIONS

Add all ingredients to a small bowl and whisk gently to combine. Place the mixture in an airtight container until ready to use.

TO USE STEAK RUB

Drizzle 2 tablespoons olive oil over 1 pound of steak, such as rib eye or New York strip. Rub ¼ cup seasoning into meat and marinate for at least 30 minutes. Grill.

sweet dreams

I would have loved to own a bakery, a Paris-in-springtime space painted pristine white and shiny black, with bud vases on each table holding a perfect single bloom. The early morning would be laced with the scent of strong black coffee, *Croque Mesdames*, or *pain au chocolat*. On the counter awaiting customers would be a zesty Pink Lemonade cake with fluffy buttercream frosting.

When I was seven or eight, I received a hand-me-down pink Easy-Bake oven, complete with mini tins and packaged fudge mix.

In childhood, I churned out teeth-achingly sweet cakes doused in sprinkles; cherry pie filling mounded in crust that tasted like cardboard, and barely baked chocolate chip cookies. None of this deterred my hungry siblings, who had been raised on homemade plain yogurt and unsweetened applesauce.

In Ms. Cairo's fourth-grade classroom, I stood at a table with a red-and-white-checkered cloth, a jam jar holding some egg-yolk-colored dandelions, and a small glass candy dish of after-dinner mints. We were to give an oral presentation about

our career of choice and at that time, I had the lofty goal to become a waitress.

I remember the wonderful glow of self-confidence I felt as the group gathered around my station. As my classmates were made comfortable in their small plastic chairs, I busied myself passing around a candy dish and handing out Dixie cups with water. My 'diners' enthusiastically sucked squares of peppermint and proceeded to discuss the latest episode of *Mork and Mindy*. Though I had outlined my dreams in loopy letters written on 3 x 5 note cards, it seemed counterproductive to interrupt them, despite the disapproving looks I was receiving from my teacher. My desire had been to cultivate a feeling of relaxed togetherness and judging from the happy voices, I had succeeded!

The bakery dream will never be a reality and my short-lived waitressing days are over. Now I find purpose and joy in everyday details, like a well-packed school lunch with a note tucked inside and a cup of Jell-O pudding as a treat or an impromptu picnic at the pond with lifelong friends. They were high school sweethearts, and we fed their gaggle of children Oscar Mayer hotdogs and made minty mojitos for ourselves.

There is a deep satisfaction in hosting dinner parties that last into the early hours. Our legs might be stretched out under the old farm-style table, or we might lounge on the back porch, cafe lights winking above with the scent of wisteria in the air.

It's comforting knowing that, though I don't entertain on a grand scale, I am reaching others. I show love in the language I speak, which is carried out in plates, platters, and bowls for those who share my circle.

SARAH

house keeping

Part magpie, I'm continually drawn to all things that possess their own magic, sparkle, and mystique.

I am aware this season causes me to rush about — accumulating, discarding, and tearing into home improvement projects with renewed zeal. Paint swatches and design ideas swirl around me. This heightened desire to re-create myself and our house reaches fever pitch as the sun gains strength and the days stretch out. Perhaps making a home cozy is a bit like a bird's innate urges after all.

I am always on the lookout for a shiny bauble to freshen the nest and a special little something that will bring just the right touch of uniqueness to a room.

I had a conversation with my cousin, Lenora, recently, in which we spoke about our emotional attachments to objects in our environments. Obviously, these things are not alive, yet they still serve to comfort us. Did we have beautiful pieces in our childhood houses? We came to the conclusion that our homes were furnished for maximum durability and minimal use of space. We kids occupied most of the square footage!

Perhaps that is also part of the infatuation for our grandmother Bernice's house. My favorite memory of this hacienda house was its cool dim interior. She was always dressed in one of her many pastel velour tracksuits, soft blonde hair freshly styled from her weekly salon appointment and signature Roman gold coin bracelet clinking.

As she pointed out the huge painting of muted desert scenes created by my vibrant, vivacious, and talented aunt and her only daughter who was tragically taken from her in a mudslide, Grandma paused for a moment with a far-off look and patted the frame's edge. "You know your aunt was so beautiful; she had an incredible energy about her. I think it's captured in the brush strokes on this canvas."

She furnished her hacienda with needlepoint chair cushions and pictures of painted forget-me-nots and primroses above the guest bed, the backing of which was that of a Civil War newspaper. I was inspired to create a powder room as she had with its deep green tiled tub, white soft-shag, and a gold seat pulled up to a vanity holding coral lipsticks, face powder and an oversized puff, and her signature scent Shalimar in a brilliant blue bottle. All this femininity was enclosed in this softly lit bathroom that spoke of another era where grooming and understated stylishness were everyday routines.

Grandma was the epitome of class and elegance; she was both thoughtful and direct, carrying herself with confidence and pride in the home she had created for her family, and for all who were lucky enough to be her guest. Grandma taught me about treasuring my dwelling space: I can feel her imprint in my own home designed with a nod to the classic, with whimsy and a mingling of old and new to create a warm, welcoming, comfortable space where the garden breaks the boundaries of home and home creeps into the garden.

This fascination in design details has led to many reincarnations of our home over the years. Many moons ago, Farmer K wallpapered the entryway and our living-dining room. I suppose it would be called a 'great room' now, but when it was built, it was meant to conserve space and materials. Though I have loved the pattern and coziness the paper created, lately it seems safe and predictable. Just because something made you exclaim with joy at one point, doesn't mean it must remain in place forever. I cautiously broached this subject with the husband over the last few months, and each time was met with exaggerated sighs and reasons why this was a bad idea.

One sunshiny day in spring, out came the vinegar water, sponges, and putty scraper, along with drop cloths, a plastic garbage bag and a stepstool. I soon found that wallpaper removal is not easy, nor is it for the faint of heart. My flight of fancy quickly became a plodding meditation, one peeling piece at a time.

Alas, at this writing, the transformation has yet to be completed. While I have the vision, Farmer K has the brute strength and knowledge gleaned from years of farming — and facing situations that required improvisation and thinking outside the box. It soon became quite clear that I required his expertise if this project was to be completed during my lifetime. After sharing my ideas and bringing out the magazine clippings that I had saved, along with pictures of the chosen ceiling light (yes, it's brushed gold and gleaming), he grudgingly came around to the idea of renewing this tired, outdated room.

I will admit, there was definitely a moment when I questioned my sanity. But now that we are on the same flight pattern and change is in the air, I am buoyed by this excursion. Souls lifted and putty knives in hand, we are winging our way forward together!

SARAH

SUMMER

picnic time

The annual 4th of July church picnic was held at the Beckmanns' prune farm. It was a stately house from the early 1900s, painted crisp white with black trim. There was a tree lined drive and the yard was enclosed with tidy boxwood hedges. Hydrangeas, ferns, and a tall stand of old fir trees created a shaded woodland landscape.

When we were children, and into our teenage years, we looked forward to this event, but not one of us thought about what went into hosting such a crowd. There were orchards and lawns to be mowed, pine needles to rake, and Adirondack chairs needed scrubbing. Checkered tablecloths were thrown over the row of picnic tables. Five-gallon water coolers were filled with lemonade or water for our refreshment.

We tramped in, totally oblivious … excited to see friends again, swim, roast hotdogs, and join in a rowdy baseball game in the back forty. At nightfall, we would run like wild under the trees while playing a competitive game of capture-the-flag. Exhausted, we piled into our family's van and trundled home, sleepy, dusty, and sticky, with the residue of roasted marshmallows on fingertips and lips. Never once did we think of the cleanup tasks left behind for the host family. There would be chairs to rearrange, large cooler and tea dispensers to clean and store away, and mud room toilets to sanitize. All this, yet they would open their property again, regardless of the lack of acknowledgment or reciprocation.

SARAH

family road tripping

It's sometime before five in the morning — that pre-dawn freshness is something I vividly remember. A hushed excitement runs below the surface as duffle bags and scuffed luggage are heaved into the back of the waiting van alongside the picnic cooler.

Our Dad does the rundown:

> *House windows shut (check).*
> *Stove and coffee pot off (check).*
> *Front and back door locked (check).*

And the headcount: Amber, Sarah, Beth, Mary, Stuart, Rachel, Carol, Ginny, Jon, Keith (it was 1986 and youngest siblings Arwen and Eleanor were not yet born). Then it's wheels down, as off we set into the wild, wild West.

The newness of the adventure has worn off by the time we reached Ashland, Oregon. Someone is pushing on someone else's seat. There's a squabble over *Tin Tin* books, hunger, and the need to pee. At our first rest stop, we pile out to potty, run the uneven paths through the sweet pines and eventually gather at the picnic table. Mom spreads peanut butter and honey on whole-wheat, and passes out juice boxes.

Back in the saddle once again, we settled in for the duration like seasoned travelers, lost in our own worlds as the scenery rolls by our windows, capturing our imaginations. Day smudges into night, the yellow lines continue to flash past and the engine gobbles up the miles. There are rest areas, truck stops, and

Denny's restaurants; each encounter is accompanied by silent counting as we file past like a little line of ants.

We descended on Uncle Joey and Aunt Carmen's house in Texas like a blight of locusts, pungent with sweat and the scent of unwashed hair and halitosis from three long days on the road and too short a time to address hygiene. Their door was always thrown open wide with extended relatives spilling out to greet us. Days that followed held barbecues, guitar strumming, and lessons in swing steps, accompanied by the background drone of cicadas.

> We would fly down the dusty back roads with gravel kicking up in the hole in the floorboards of a pickup truck, shake out skates to dispel cockroaches in an abandoned rink, prop open the doors to let in filtered sunlight and, if the gods were with us, a breeze.

Evening would find us sipping sweet tea or Big Red cola, legs sticking to the couch, bodies wedged between my Grandma B. and my Aunt Trib, while attempting to find relief from the heat in front of the spitting swamp cooler. I was forever in awe that the adults could sip hot coffee and smoke cigarettes in this inferno.

Not only were we introduced to the music of George Strait, Johnny Cash, and Alan Jackson on these trips outside our familiar world of Bach and Beethoven, but also white bread, bologna, tripe, liver and onions, and Bud Light. The kitchen with its high ceiling was muggy and close, the scent of hot oil and pinto beans bubbling on the stove added the shimmer of heat so intense you could almost see it. If a breeze blew at all through the open windows or the squeaking screen door, it was only a puff of dry wind and did nothing to cool the interior.

Yet the conversation was lively with the radio tuned to the local country station, and an occasional two-step dance move incorporated in the maneuvering that took place as many hands prepared the meals. My aunts and grandma would make stacks of tortillas, all soft, chewy, and oozing butter. The family cooks also concocted spicy corn tamales, with seasoned pork and served with a fresh salsa that brought tears to our eyes. We ate watermelon sprinkled with salt and drank sweet iced tea. We congregated on the back porch, listening to the twang of country tunes sung by our uncles as they strummed guitars and wailed on harmonicas. Swatting at mosquitoes while breathing in air carrying the scent of Marlboro Lights and beer, we were deliriously elated with the worldliness of it all!

Pondering this now in my grown-up mind, I wonder where we slept. How many routines were disrupted as we wandered from one day to the next, entertained and fed? It was obvious that money was tight, but my uncles and aunts never let on that the extra work or expense was a burden. We all chatted in the dimly lit rooms, fans whirring, the clatter of dishes a background hymn to their cheerful voices. We were being shaped, exposed, educated without words in the ritual of hospitality. It's not what you have, but how you use it. Here were the loaves and fishes Biblical story in action, an act of love and faith and unfailing devotion to family. This was an example of our roots and the actions we should strive to emulate.

It's odd, but I can't remember the long drive home.

SARAH

a sister comes to visit

A bead of sweat trickles down between my shoulder blades as I stop hoeing to take a cool drink of water. Squinting at the sun riding high in the sky, I step into the shade of the willow tree to catch a few moments of cool. I barely disturb a brightly plumed rooster that had settled in for an afternoon nap. I watch as a hen party ambles by, feeling a sense of envy at their acceptance of a slower pace to match the dog days of summer. A dry wind kicks up and the sound of a thousand rustling leaves joins the quiet slush-slushing of the irrigation driplines and the low murmur of bees and bugs as they bumble on their way.

One of my sisters and her family are coming to stay the weekend, and my mind is racing with all the things that need to be accomplished before they arrive. Returning to the chore at hand, dust plumes up as I hurriedly run the hoe over the weeds; one more row and the garden will be checked off the list.

> I don't know why I feel like I have to manicure the yard and make the house sparkle with cleanliness.

In my heart I know I need to find a balance between immaculate and lived in. There was a motto in our childhood home: Many hands make little work, and it is true. It also means I will have to let go of my idea of perfection as I have far fewer appendages working through the list of chores than we had in the large family of my childhood.

The air is hot and heavy as I hang wet cotton sheets from the guest beds on the line. The feel of the cool crisp dampness against my skin brings momentary relief from the heat. Tired hands fumble with the clothespins and my thoughts still and settle. This has to be one of the most relaxing duties of the day. Looking out over the flower garden, I see the cows grazing lazily in the pasture as a hawk surfs the current of air above.

It's days like this when the home and garden dance in perfect harmony. I am overcome with the feeling of contentment, regardless of the amount of care they take.

My little boy comes up to me, tugging on my skirt. "Mama, Mama look at this worm — I found it by the pond can I keep it?"

I smile, spit saliva on my thumb as my mother used to do, and rub his dirty cheek, exposing the freckles underneath. He grimaces and squirms away.

"I think the worm would miss his home, don't you?" Nodding reluctantly, he heads off to return it to the murky banks as I call after him to wash his hands, as his cousins will be here soon.

An old song comes to me from my childhood when I was little enough to still require a chair to stand on next to my mother at the sink. Her dress was sage green and dark hair was pulled back in a simple twist. I remember thinking how beautiful she was as her voice hummed the tune, occasionally softly singing a phrase or two. I do so now as I carry the empty basket to the back porch.

"Hello the house!"

A big smile greets me as I rush to meet my sister and her family at the front door and the home explodes with loud chatter, loads of sleeping bags, luggage, and children galloping about in excitement.

After settling in and herding the kids outside to play, I pour
two glasses of iced tea and take my sister's arm. Slipping by our
husbands who are deep in conversation on the back porch,
we wander out into the gardens.

We gush over the roses, dahlias, and sunflowers
while watching the butterflies dancing among
the lavender.

Moving on to the vegetable patch lush with runner beans,
cucumbers, and tomatoes, we chat recipes and canning
techniques.

In the orchard, gnarled apple and pear trees are heavy-laden
with fruit soon to ripen. We wander into the little greenhouse at
the back, where inside terra-cotta pots are filled with succulents,
scented lemon trees, and exotic orchids passed down from our
grandmother. Settling into the two lawn chairs just outside,
our conversation turns to life, husbands and children, stretching
a budget, and how gardens are sanity-savers in a chaotic world.

Next on the agenda is dinner preparation. Both of us agree it
must be memorable for the kiddos. Plans are made for a bonfire
and marshmallow roast this evening. I've made strawberry
rhubarb crisp ahead of time, which will be perfect for adults,
though I have yet to meet a person who can pass-up a blackened
blob of confection at the end of a stick!

We call the boys to take charge and soon whittling knives are
pulled from pockets and shavings fly as the crackling fire comes
to life. The girls grab clippers and head to the garden to pick a
bouquet for the table. Giggling and tripping over each other,
they scamper off, eager to make a beautiful creation. My sister

turns to me and notes that this was us not so long ago.

We stand still with our hands intertwined as if to hold onto this moment. Soon we make our way out to the garden with platters piled high. It's a procession that includes a large bowl of watermelon wedges, a steaming corn casserole, crunchy cilantro-lime coleslaw, and an assortment of hotdog fixings in a basket. Bringing up the rear is a young one carefully holding a tin tray loaded with marshmallows, dark chocolate squares, and some packets of graham crackers.

We will have a feast tonight to celebrate the summer's bounty and the gift of being able to share our spot in the universe with family!

The sun is giving over its place in the sky. All falls quiet as plates are loaded and food is enjoyed. The chef of the hour is beaming with pride over his culinary skills as he settles a pan loaded with perfectly charred drumsticks and thighs, all sticky sweet and smothered in blackberry barbecue sauce, on the table as the recipients ooh and aah.

Dusk sets in as the bonfire burns low and steady, crickets sing, and the winds from the Van Duzer Corridor cool the air. I top up glasses with the last of the wine and settle back into my chair. Our youngest, shirtless, with sagging dirty jeans, rests his head on my shoulder, feeling left out. I call for his sister and she tells him to stop being a ninny and come back to hear ghost stories.

The children are lined in a row on the back porch as I sit with my sister, conversing in low tones. Soft music flows from the kitchen. A full moon has risen, lighting the garden in a cool

white glow and a lone owl swoops soundlessly overhead.

I am filled with gratitude for the simple things so often taken for granted and reminded yet again that joy lies not in perfection, but in sharing and connecting. A full life means embracing time and using it in the presence of those you love.

BETH

blackberry barbecue sauce

SERVINGS: 2 CUPS

When summer air is thick with heat and the lazy buzz of pollinators, our flip-flops kick up mini-dust storms as we walk along a firebreak. The destination is the wild patch of juicy blackberries hanging plump and seductive on their thorny vines. When smeared on tender barbecued chicken, this sweet-sticky concoction is the perfect accompaniment to a summer's day.

PREP TIME: 10 minutes

COOK TIME: 15 minutes

INGREDIENTS

3 cups fresh or frozen and thawed blackberries

½ cup apple cider vinegar

¾ cup brown sugar

¼ cup Crowley House honey, or any local honey

1 cup ketchup

2 tablespoons Worcestershire sauce

1 teaspoon ground dry mustard

½ teaspoon chili powder

½ teaspoon onion powder

1 teaspoon ground mustard

¼ teaspoon dried thyme

Salt and pepper to taste

INSTRUCTIONS

Combine ingredients in a medium saucepan; stir to combine. Bring to a simmer and reduce to low heat. Continue to simmer, stirring constantly until mixture thickens-approximately 15 minutes. Use a basting brush to coat chicken prior to grilling.

cilantro-lime coleslaw

SERVES: 7

When we first tasted this delicious slaw, it was an incredibly hot day full of baseball playoffs. The team moms set out the between-game potluck bowls of pasta salad, bags of Doritos, and ball-park buns onto a rickety foldout table in a scant slice of shade. This light slaw provides a flavorful take on a normally ho-hum contribution. It has been our one and only slaw ever since, proving to be a home-run hit — whether served as a side or to top a pulled-pork slider. Feel free to add a cup of shredded red cabbage to jazz up the presentation.

PREP TIME: 25 minutes

INGREDIENTS

¾ cup real mayonnaise

1 lime, zested

2 teaspoons fresh lime juice

½ teaspoon rice vinegar

2 cloves garlic minced

2 teaspoons sweet chili sauce

2 teaspoons white sugar

3 tablespoons finely chopped fresh cilantro

¼ cup red onion, finely diced

4 cups shredded green or red cabbage, or more to taste

INSTRUCTIONS

Whisk mayonnaise, lime zest, lime juice, rice vinegar, garlic, sweet chili sauce, and sugar in a large bowl, stirring until sugar is dissolved. Mix in cilantro and red onion. Add cabbage, about 1 cup at a time, making sure it is all coated. Serve.

corn casserole

SERVES: 6-8

Are we the only ones at potlucks and family gatherings who have one eye on the activities and the other on our contribution to the food table? We know self-worth and acceptance should not be equated with a bowl scraped clean, and the desire of the reward of an empty dish at the end of the meal. You can confidently bring this casserole to your next gathering; it won't disappoint, and you will be graciously accepting compliments all evening!

PREP TIME: 5 minutes

INGREDIENTS

32 ounces fresh or frozen corn, thawed

½ cup mayonnaise

½ cup sour cream

1 ½ teaspoons chili powder, I prefer chipotle powder

½ teaspoon garlic powder

½ teaspoon kosher salt

¼ teaspoon cayenne

5 oz. crumbled *queso fresco* (Mexican cheese)

¼ cup fresh cilantro, chopped

INSTRUCTIONS

Pour corn into a 8 x 8 casserole dish. In a small bowl combine mayonnaise, sour cream, chili powder, garlic powder, kosher salt, and half the *queso fresco*, and stir until combined. Pour over corn and mix until all kernels are coated. Bake uncovered for 30-40 minutes or until heated through and the edge begins to bubble and brown. Remove from the oven. Sprinkle the casserole with remaining cheese and fresh cilantro and serve.

less ethel more lucy

It was not uncommon to find mom and dad dancing in the kitchen, with his arms around her waist and cheek pressed against her hair; they inhabited a world of their own. Meanwhile the pasta water boiled full tilt on the stove, and the young ones snaked like a thrashing dragon's tail through the crowded kitchen space.

Once I became queen of my own domain, I didn't emulate this blissful culinary scene. For years my demands and rigidity for order and timeliness gave off a decisive schoolmarmish vibe with lists of schedules and ingredients tacked to the fridge. I was convinced this method of control was the standard by which my efficiency and worth was measured. I often was run ragged in a race wherein I was always competing against myself. This was one I could never hope to win.

Thankfully life intervened: a chronically sick child, sports schedules, and a broadening circle of friends in the same stages of upheaval led to a loosening of the reins. Becoming less Ethel and more Lucy taught me to relax and enjoy the process and adventure of of it all. Out with hors d'oeuvres-through-dessert perfection and guests banished to the living room while I scurried and fretted. In with the signature cocktail that immediately put everyone at ease, an option to pick up a knife and join in the menu preparation, or to just hang out in the kitchen and chat. Congo lines have been known to cha-cha through my cooking space and the actual time for sitting down to supper is anyone's guess. But with this acceptance of an unpretentious attitude came the realization that life and love through the expression of food is truly a dance to be savored.

SARAH

love & marriage

The winding road feels endless as I drive home from a wedding held across the valley. With the windows rolled down and wind rushing in, the air brings the warm scent of blackberries ripening on the vine and layers of dust. I drive past fields of wheat as a rolling sea of gold stretches up and crests over the hills. Open spaces of neatly clipped acres, void of its harvested grass crop, are now punctuated with straw bales waiting to be stored. A red barn, standing tall, is still impressive despite fading paint and missing shingles. The sun is sinking low, casting shadows through the trees. As a child, I remember riding along in the maxi van on our Sunday evening drives, our parents' inexpensive way of entertaining 12 young children. The little ones closest to the windows would hold outstretched arms, flying along as mom led us in one of the many ditties from the soundtrack to our childhood:

> *Mairzy doates and dozy doates and liddle lamzy divey*
> *A kiddlely divey too, wouldn't you?*

The countryside was where our mother was most at peace. Those wide-open plains of her Texas home with its sagebrush, prairie grasses, and bluebonnets as far as the eye could see never relinquished their hold on her heart. We could sense she missed home and the family she'd left behind for our father when she would get that far-off look in her eyes.

As a flower farmer and florist, much of my work revolves around weddings and the emotions tied to marriage. Today was no exception. Five o'clock in the morning found me perking coffee and looking over the print-out of the upcoming event yet again. The list reads as follows:

Bridal Bouquet: Antique vibe, soft, flowing, dusty rose, mustard yellows, long ribbon

Bridesmaids: (4) Same as above but smaller. Short ribbon

Boutonnières: Groom + 4 groomsmen. Father of bride, father of groom, officiant, 2 ushers. Smaller version for ring bearer

Wrist corsages: Mother of the bride, mother of the groom

Rose petals in bag for flower girl

2 large arrangements for wine barrels at entrance

2 hanging floral pieces for arch

3 buckets of assorted blooms for bud vases on tables

Zip ties, wire, clippers, and flowers to bedeck horse-drawn carriage

I make my way in the cool morning air to the studio with my coffee, activate Spotify, and slip into the creative zone. I change the water in each of the containers, recutting the ends of bouquets, then wrapping them in satin ribbon, secured with pearled push pins. I retrieve boutonnières from the cooler, and spritz them with holding formula before tucking them into a carrier box with the corsages.

Other floral creations are nestled in tissue paper and settled into transport boxes for the ride to the venue. Step ladders, water bottles, energy bars, canvas bag with essentials . . . check, check, check. I change quickly into a simple black dress and sandals, apply a swipe of brilliant red lipstick and a dash of mascara, and off I go.

The Grange, one of hundreds in Oregon, is tucked between the hills, wedged back at the end of a long dirt road surrounded by tall Pin oak trees. The grass is tightly mowed and crispy brown in the late summer sun. This aging building is a white clapboard structure, edges trimmed with matte black. The tall, narrow windows still hold the original wavy glass in the panes. Through double doors comes the clatter and laughter of a group of family and friends who have worked these events together often.

The mood is relaxed and comfortable as they assemble food in the open kitchen. Making my way across the worn wood floors, I set up my station on the stage and begin the final preparations. I am frantic-focused. As often as I do this, there is always a feeling of anticipation and urgency until all arrangements are placed, arches hung, and the bride's happy reaction to her flowers noted.

Later, the ceremony concluded, picnic tables are ladened with pulled pork, crunchy coleslaw, homemade rolls, and a wide assortment of sweet treats made by adoring aunts are on offer. The music and atmosphere feels giddy as I slide into a seat next to the young groom's mother. She is watching the wedding party stomping out a line dance with misty eyes. Inevitably, I hear what I almost always hear,

"This is good, right? They look so happy! We gave them the wedding they dreamed of . . ."

Yes. Yes. Yes. And so much more.

I drive the last few miles down our dirt road to the old farmhouse and my gardens. Above, the sky is peach and brilliant orange, and the air is beginning to cool. The screen door closes behind me and I kick off my sandals. There's an evening glow streaming in the windows and dust fairies are dancing along with the tunes coming from the kitchen. I stop to pet the cat that has come to greet me, her fur soft against my bare legs, the vibration of her purring bearing a welcome.

My other-half calls from the kitchen that dinner is ready and wine is poured for me. There's a peck on the cheek as I enter and accept the chilled glass of Pinot Gris.

Moving past him to the garden, he pats my bum with a twinkle in his eye. The days of young love is captured in that one millisecond.

I remember standing in the early morning light on my parents' front porch, gazing out at the small gathering of family in white folding chairs clustered in the grass.

The thought that ran through my head as I made my way towards the smiling faces was — that this was bigger than buying my truck!

That it was. There have been joy rides and slow wanders, breakdowns, and moments of left-on-the-side-of-the-road-for-dead. The way has been bumpy at times, then smooth and open for miles; there have been hot nights of steamy parking, and cold stretches of icy silence. Yet, through dogged determination and sheer will, our marriage loops around, picking us up, carrying us on to another adventure together.

BETH

AUTUMN

fall's golden hour

The golden hour of fall, that flirtatious passing, the gentle brush of one season against another. The sun's lingering gaze warms the earth for just a few more moments before surrendering his space to the moon. In the deepening dusk a skein of geese flies by, a tight wedge, militant and purposeful in their quest for shelter from the coming storm. I feel a twinge of envy, a desire for freedom, adventure, a life where danger haunts the edge of my days and nightfall might find me on a foreign shore.

The wind has kicked up sending leaves skittering by. A chill shakes my body as I wake from a daydream and pull my well-worn flannel shirt closer around me.

Quickening my pace, I set out to finish the harvest before the rain arrives.

I straighten up at the end of the row, hands cold, chapped, and stained with dirt, my bones aching as I move to the next line of cabbages; just a few more to gather tonight.

I must collect the last of the tomatoes, too. I feel my body lagging from a long growing season, tears spring up and ride hot behind my eyelids. I draw in a deep breath and slowly exhale, suppressing that overwhelmed feeling for a little while longer.

Lights in the farmhouse cast a warm glow over the gardens and
my heart yearns for the quieter phases of winter, which will soon
be upon us. Days where there's fire crackling and the ticking
clock reminds us that we have nowhere to go, and all day to get
there. Gathering up a few more buckets of vegetables, I make
my way to the barn. Like a horse heading for home, my steps fall
in line as if I'm almost marching, purposeful in my quest for a
well-stocked larder. The barn is cool and musky, smelling of dirt
and old beams, age, and evening air. I fill in the last few spaces
on the bottom shelf with deep purple cabbages, then lean down,
grabbing a few slatted bins into which I begin to load carrots,
turnips, and beets, tucking them into the cool dirt.

I stretch my stiff neck from side to side, closing my eyes for a
moment. A small hand taps me on the shoulder and I open my
eyes to see an impish grinning face. I smile and grab my little one
into a much-needed hug, using my apron to wipe the smudges of
grime I had deposited on his forehead. I kiss his soft, rosy cheeks
as he giggles and squirms.

"Mama, can I help?" We work alongside each other, and my
thoughts turn to the years ahead when he will take this work
ethic into his own life. I show him how to set each root vegetable
in, stacking and covering until all are snug beneath their earth
blanket.

"All righty, then. That's done. Time for dinner!" I say.

He slips his hand in mine. I close up for the day, and we head to
the warmth of home. As we walk, I think of the most precious
of all the gifts my garden has given me — hope for the future,
the seasons to come, and a validation of a job well done. We are
sustained by beauty and produce.

BETH

preserving the garden

It's the season of preserving and preparing our larder for the cold, dark days of winter.

My mother called my name when it was my turn to help in the kitchen. With a smile, I climbed up on the stool and took my place next to her. It was so important to my mother to spend time with each of us; it was how she could show her love, and it was all we needed. I recall the simple times with her, like grocery shopping with a twenty-five-cent piece tucked into my hand for a little treat; or I might head off to the meat locker to wander the dark maze, until we found our number and gathered the frozen goods for the week.

That day, we canned up some fresh-picked peaches from the tree in the garden. My job was to pack the peach slices into the jar with my little hand. My mother's ever-watchful eyes and kind smile kept order in the kitchen.

Fall was busy in our little home. I think back to how our mother kept all of us in line with all the work that had to be done, a baby in a pack, toddlers and young ones gathered at her skirts, and we older ones "helping" probably too much, but nonetheless she found patience, training us to keep home, bless others, and find grace.

Today, decades later, I'm canning peaches from Crowley House Farm orchard. I ladle in the hot, lightly sweetened syrup over the golden peaches. With bubbles rising, I push the peaches down tightly and their fresh smell fills the kitchen. My son hands me another jar, ready to load; my daughter places the lids and rings.

My husband keeps an eye on the canner, ready for the next batch. I know it doesn't sound like much, but this simple form of entertainment fills me with joy. Having my family gathered in the kitchen with a common vision of preserving the bounty, I know I'm passing on a tradition. My arms full of jars, I set them in a neat row on the pantry shelf and the colors of the season pop from green beans and tomatoes to chutneys and jams. I place the peaches next to the applesauce, and stand back to admire the beauty of it all.

> With so much work put into this colorful pantry display, I know I could have run to the store to buy conventional alternatives, but it would have not been the same.

There is just something about homegrown goodness that sustains you, and there is a sense of security and peace of mind in knowing you have provided for your family food with unmatched quality.

As my children grow, I find that passing on this old way of doing things has been one of my most rewarding accomplishments as a mother. I love teaching not just my daughter, but also my son, to keep house; to use what you have to create beautiful food with thought, no matter the time of year. It's about taking pride in the garden, the animals you raise, the environment you create in the home with simple decor from the garden. Most important, it's about the act of sharing the bounty with others, as my mother taught me. She always had a "welcome, come in and sit awhile" mug of coffee poured, and a plate of food set before you.

BETH

mizzle

A light rain or drizzle. That misty dampness that saturates the leaves and clings to air particles, making its way into clothes, seeming to cross the boundaries of skin to seep into your very bones. Fall in the Northwest comes on suddenly; one moment we are basking in golden light and warmth of the lingering summer, and in the next, great gusts of wind toss the bright leaves to the ground with abandon. The air becomes heavy with the earthy-peaty smell of decaying foliage and rain drenched soil.

Though never ready for the darkness to return, we Oregonians acclimate quickly. It's muck-boots and Pendleton wool jackets; beanie caps and patterned scarves. We break out our assortment of tights and sweaters that have been stored under beds or in closets. There's a certain gleeful expectation as the days grow short, and the inky blackness presses itself against windowpanes before the clock turns to four in the afternoon.

> The outside world becomes damp and dismal,
> as our cocoon inside grows warm and glowing.

Tartan plaid blankets and nubby throws hang over couches and on arms of chairs. The fire glows in the living room hearth, and rust-colored candles flicker on the dining room table. I prefer an Edison bulb and the ambiance it creates, causing the boys to joke, "Hey, can someone turn on a light? Oh, wait, it's on already!" Its amber hues soothe and flatter to such a degree that I put up with their kindhearted teasing and the occasional eye strain.

Fall food offers another level of comfort. Braised cuts of meat all caramelized in saucy tomato goodness, peppery arugula tossed with earthy roasted beets, toasted pecans, and crumbled mild goat cheese coated with a light vinaigrette, is an all time favorite. I'm a sucker for bread in any form. If greeted with hunks of chewy, whole-grain slathered with butter, or slices of thick crusty sourdough and a side of seasoned olive oil, your wish is my command. Split pea soup and hearty stews find their way to the weeknight table, delightful for both their tummy-warming qualities, and their ease of reheating.

We love desserts in winter: pear crisp with mounds of slightly sweet whipped cream riding on the crunchy crust of oatmeal and brown sugar, spice cakes served with strong Earl Gray tea or a dense, fudgy bittersweet chocolate cookie sprinkled with sea salt make the dark days less dreadful.

Winding down, snuggling in, curling up. These are movements our bodies remember from past years and even anticipate after the long of summer.

Leaves fall, and there's a tangle of bare branches above us; birds wing south in crisp formation. Our bodies, along with the earth, let out an almost audible sigh of settling. Outside, garden tools and farm machinery are put away in sheds and barns to winter over snug and dry. Books are dusted off from shelves and fill baskets alongside comfy chairs as permission is granted to just be.

We are creatures of the natural world; seeking shelter in the nest and burrows we call home. We welcome the coming chill, knowing the decay and rain will recharge the earth as the additional downtime will be the rest our bodies have been craving.

SARAH

roasted beet salad

SERVES: 4

This salad is the perfect crossover, swinging us from summer to fall with earthy flavors of root vegetables and toasted nuts over crisp baby greens, mellow cheese, and a bright vinaigrette.

PREP TIME: 15 minutes

COOK TIME: 1 hour

PREHEAT oven to 375 degrees F

INGREDIENTS

3 bunches small to medium cooked beets (8-10 beets)

3 tablespoons olive oil

½ red onion, thinly sliced

6 cups baby salad greens (greens, spinach or arugula)

½ cup coarsely chopped toasted walnuts or pecans

½ cup crumbled plain goat cheese

BEETS

Use an assortment of colors, trim tops, and scrub well.

Place in a roasting pan and drizzle with olive oil; pour ½ cup water in the bottom of the pan. Cover tightly with foil and roast for at least 45 minutes up to one hour. The beets are cooked when you can easily pierce them with a fork. Let cool and peel.

While beets are roasting, make the dressing. Refrigerate until needed.

HONEY BALSAMIC DRESSING

¼ cup balsamic vinegar

¼ cup canola oil

¼ cup olive oil

2 tablespoons honey

½ cup crumbled plain goat cheese

1 tablespoon Dijon mustard

1 clove garlic-minced

¾ teaspoon of sea salt, and pepper to taste

ASSEMBLE THE SALAD

Place the fresh arugula or greens on a platter and top with the marinated beets and onion, toasted walnuts, and crumbled goat cheese. Drizzle with additional dressing. Serve immediately.

harvest memories

The Dietrich house could be reached by squirming through the hole we had dug under the fence behind our fort in the back corner of the garden. As this was unacceptable, according to our mother, fall found us spit-shined and freshly braided, trooping down the road and turning left, as we made our way in civilized fashion to the front door of the old two-story farmhouse.

The home stood at the end of a long drive flanked with massive pine trees. It was a dwelling place for crows creating a ruckus each evening, which fed our overactive imaginations, already stimulated by countless stories of forest fairies, talking creatures, and evil witches. In choked-out sunlight we shivered with fear, yet the excitement propelled us forward, up the front steps to the covered porch where we bunched behind Mom like a pile of wriggling puppies.

Mrs. Dietrich always invited us in for treats in her cozy yellow kitchen with its faded wallpaper and worn linoleum floors. Though my memories are vague, the feeling and smells remain: long hallways cast in shadows, a mossy green-colored living room with welcoming, deep-cushioned couches, and a ticking mantel clock. At the end of our visit, Mr. Dietrich would trundle along behind us as we made our way homeward, pushing a large wheelbarrow loaded with gnarled hubbards, striped delicatas, smooth butternuts and deep green acorn squash, plus a few long sturdy stocks of Brussels sprouts and mammoth cabbages — fall bounty from his prolific garden. After stacking his offering on the covered back porch, he would flash his toothless grin and shyly wave as he turned for home. In our eyes, he was a gnome from a fairytale who, once a year, traveled here from his world.

SARAH

a place of peace

I prefer a welcoming, well lived-in environment that suggests children have left chocolate fingerprints on the lower levels of door frames. Fluffy friends lounge on dining room chairs, safely away from those who would return them to the great outdoors. A place where pantry shelves are filled with baking ingredients stored with no apparent rhyme or reason, and pot and pans are stacked hodge-podge behind cabinet doors.

> We adore a deep, comfortable sofa.
> Whether clothed in crushed velvet or corduroy, it
> must be bedecked with the perfect amount
> of assorted throw pillows.

Couches need to invite people to wriggle down and borrow a book from the stack that is listing against the wall. Better yet, the occupant can wrap themselves in a woolly blanket and curl up to drift off into dreamland.

The best compliment I ever received was from a bride's mother. After spending time on the back porch talking flower colors and cake flavors, we walked through the house and she said, "Oh,

I could sit on your sofa and just take in this room for hours!"

That is exactly how I feel.

A dwelling is a place of peace, of interest and intrigue, a collection of bits and pieces of our lives. Stories told that cannot be manufactured, but instead come from a collection curated by wanderings, friendships, experiences, and adventures.

> A home catches and enfolds one at the end of the day. It's where shoes are slipped off and purses and keys are shed on the entryway table.

Binding waistbands and bras that dig into rib cages or slip from shoulders are discarded for Snuggies and thick socks. Wine is sloshed into stemless glasses and feet are tucked up beneath us as we are swallowed into the embrace of an overstuffed chair.

Home is a smell, a feeling, a sound. It has its own heartbeat and rhythm but is also an extension of its inhabitants. It should not be created for how it will appear to others, but instead be the mothership you return to after surviving the whirlwind and chaos of these wild excursions we call our lives.

SARAH

APRIL 1970   40 CENTS

Sunset
THE MAGAZINE OF *WESTERN LIVING*

Weekend-house planners
throw away the rule book

Fresno's Super Sandwich

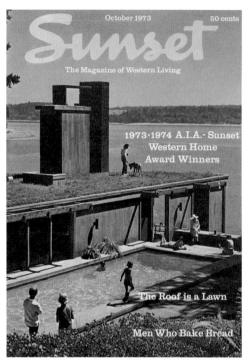

October 1973   50 cents

Sunset
The Magazine of Western Living

1973·1974 A.I.A.- Sunset
Western Home
Award Winners

The Roof is a Lawn

Men Who Bake Bread

FEBRUARY 1972   50 CENTS

Sunset
THE MAGAZINE OF *WESTERN LIVING*

Experimental
Garden in the Desert
Near Tucson

Eggs Rancheros for Lunch? Bueno!

AUGUST 1956 · 25 CENTS

Sunset
THE MAGAZINE OF *WESTERN LIVING*

Ideas for
beach houses
—
Small garden
pools

• The trees that
captured California

ode to sunset

Sunset magazine in our rural Oregon lives was a window to the outside world that lay beyond 13th Avenue with its jumble of banana-seat bicycles in the driveway out front. With photo spreads of seashores, how-to stories on macrame, and recipes for shrimp cocktail and avocado toast, it all teased of a land both familiar and foreign.

Our annual subscription was the Christmas gift from our uncle and aunt who lived in Los Angeles with cousins we barely knew, yet admired greatly. They were cool to our klutz, worldly-wise to our sheltered existence; envied, admired and adored from afar. As fraternal twins, the boy was tall and dashing with movie star looks and charisma, while his sister was petite and beautiful, possessing an infectious laugh. They rocked the feathered hair, wore buckle-back jeans and sported funky jewelry. Wheels consisted of a retro Mustang for him, and a zippy sporty foreign car for her. No using the family van to get a driver's permit for them, no siree!

> *Sunset* promised equal allure, its monthly articles piquing our curiosity, for its content, and for the context of who sent it to us.

Filled with photos of A-framed houses decorated so differently from ours, swanky boulevards and quaint shops, surfers and organic farmers, majestic redwood forests and desolate deserts — the magazine was a tapestry of tantalizing adventure and a porthole to an alternate life.

Today, copies of the magazine are ever-present on the coffee table and kitchen counter. In 2021, *Sunset* published "Farmer John's Favorite Pumpkin Bread," from Eda Muller at Farmer John's Farm. It is spicy, cake-like in texture, and full of toasted nuts and plump raisins. It is breakfast for the week and, when buttered, a one-hand meal on the run.

SARAH

farmer john's favorite pumpkin bread

SERVES: 2 loaves, about 10 slices each

TOTAL PREP TIME: 15 minutes

COOK TIME: 50-60 minutes

PREHEAT oven to 350 degrees F

INGREDIENTS

2 cups all-purpose flour

1 ¼ cups firmly packed dark brown sugar

1 cup granulated sugar

1 cup coarsely chopped walnuts or pecans (lightly toast for extra crunch)

½ cup raisins

1 ½ teaspoons baking soda

1 ½ teaspoons ground cinnamon

1 ¼ teaspoons ground nutmeg

¾ teaspoons salt

¾ teaspoons ground cloves

½ teaspoons ground allspice

½ teaspoons ground ginger

3 large eggs

1 ¾ cups canned pumpkin

¾ cups vegetable oil

INSTRUCTIONS

Lightly oil two 8 ½-x-4 ½-inch loaf pans.

In a large bowl, combine flour, brown sugar, nuts, raisins, baking soda, cinnamon, nutmeg, salt, cloves, allspice, and ginger until well blended.

In a separate bowl, whisk eggs, then add mashed pumpkin and oil until well blended. Add wet ingredients to flour mixture and stir just until well blended. Pour into two lightly oiled 8 ½-x-4 ½ -inch loaf pans

Bake until bread pulls from the sides and a wooden skewer inserted in center comes out clean, about 50 to 60 minutes. Let bread cool in pans on a rack for about 15 minutes. Cut around outside edges of the bread and invert onto rack. Cool thoroughly.

the 9x13 casserole

Circle the wagons, pull up the drawbridge, hunker down. Regroup, recharge, recover. This is what we do when life-altering events occur, and the future seems daunting.

It could come in the form of a new baby, skin silky soft and still carrying the scent of the mystical land from whence it has just traveled. Or perhaps a torn ankle tendon from a misstep off an unimpressive height of approximately four inches. The heartache of a job loss or missing puppy also qualifies, as do breakups and poor scores on a much-studied-for exam.

> The greatest loss, that of a loved one,
> prompts the deepest reaction, an almost visceral
> need to cream sugar and butter into a sweet,
> soothing concoction.

To take meat and sear it, layering it in tomato paste and rich red wine, cooking it for hours with a bouquet of thyme, oregano, and rosemary, letting the herbs infuse themselves and their healing powers into every drop of sauce. We believe in using our powers for good, creating the spell of comfort in a enamel casserole as its aroma permeates the home of our loved ones.

Even those of us who prefer to suffer in solitude crawl out from under a man-made den of covers to accept a lasagna stuffed with Italian sausage and smothered in a mixture of provolone and mozzarella cheese, or the family-sized chicken enchilada.

With overwhelming thoughts of gratitude for those offering the casserole to us, we find the strength to stand again. It is this hope, when the tables are turned, that propels us into uncharted water as we reach out to others who are floundering or sinking in situations that feel out of their depth, offering our hearts in the guise of a hot dish covered in a kitchen cloth.

When terminal cancer hits your inner circle, the world wobbles madly and slips off its axis. This happens suddenly and violently; for us, it was a cloudless day in May when the diagnosis hurtled at us, causing unbearable disbelief and a fervent wish to wake up from the nightmare, for storm clouds to clear, and life to be normal once again.

More than a brother-in-law, Wayne was part of the structure supporting this family since our sister was fifteen and fell madly in love with a blonde, curly-haired cowboy from Montana. Always our rudder, he was the stillness below the waves, our sister's steady and unseen force maneuvering this sometimes-listing ship through storms and windless stretches. He was the guest you find doing dishes when you return to the kitchen for the second pot of coffee, the hand on your shoulder when life has you feeling wonky, and the one who sent text messages of encouragement just as you thought no one noticed you exhaustedly scurrying behind the scenes.

It feels as if there's a hurricane in our path, or that we are sailing straight for a gigantic whirlpool or the ledge that marks the end of the earth. All this is looming with no chance of escape, and we must carry on without him, an outcome too staggering to comprehend.

In the words of the psychotherapist and writer, Francis Weller, "Grief and love are sisters, woven together from the beginning. Their kinship reminds us that there is no love that does not

contain loss and no loss that is not a reminder of our love we carry for what we once held close."

So, we will make comfort in the shape of a familiar casserole, all the while keeping our eyes on the horizon and hope in our hearts for that glimmer of light that speaks of a new dawn that is bound to conquer this heavy darkness.

SARAH

mom's comfort casserole

SERVES: 6-8

Fall brings on sniffles and sneezes. At the first sign of an ill breeze blowing through our house, our mother would start making recipes that allowed us to feel just a wee bit better. This casserole always did the trick with its thick, rich, meaty base and hearty vegetables, layered beneath a mound of golden mashed potatoes whipped to perfection. Mom would dish up a large spoonful on our plates, along with a side of greens, and a slice of warm bread. It was all the comfort needed to feel better!

TOTAL PREP TIME: 30 minutes

COOK TIME: 30-40 minutes

INGREDIENTS FOR MASHED POTATOES

2 pounds Yukon Gold potatoes, peeled and cut into uniform, 1-inch chunks

1 cup heavy cream

3 tablespoons unsalted butter

2 egg yolks

½ cup parmesan cheese, finely grated

1 teaspoon kosher salt

½ teaspoon black pepper

4-5 cloves garlic, peeled

1 cup cheddar cheese for topping; garnish with fresh chopped parsley

PREPARE MASHED POTATOES

In a large pot, cover potatoes and garlic cloves with cold water and bring to a boil. Lower heat to a simmer until potatoes are fork-tender. Drain well. In the same pot, melt unsalted butter. Pour in heavy cream and whisk two egg yolks into the mixture, along with salt and pepper. Stir in parmesan cheese and return potatoes and garlic cloves to the pot. Mash until light and fluffy.

INGREDIENTS FOR MEAT FILLING

1 pound ground meat (beef or lamb)

4 slices of bacon

1 teaspoon black pepper

1 ½ teaspoons kosher salt

1 large onion, finely chopped

2 cloves garlic, crushed

1 teaspoon fresh or dried rosemary

1 teaspoon fresh or dried thyme

2 large carrots, finely chopped

2 celery ribs, finely chopped

1 cup fresh or thawed frozen corn

1 cup fresh or thawed frozen peas

2 tablespoons tomato paste

2 tablespoons flour

2 tablespoons Worcestershire sauce

1 cup red wine

½ cup beef broth

PREPARE MEAT FILLING

Place a large cast iron skillet or heavy casserole over medium heat and add ground meat. Sprinkle meat with salt and pepper. Brown meat until fully cooked. Drain excess fat and put cooked meat aside in a bowl.

Chop bacon into ¼ inch pieces and fry over medium heat. Remove bacon, leaving the fat in the pan.Add chopped onions to the bacon fat and cook for 3 minutes. Add carrots and celery. Cook until vegetables are fork tender and onions are golden brown and translucent. Add garlic and cook for about 1 minute.

Add meat and bacon back into the pan alongside the onions and vegetables. Add in flour, tomato paste, wine, and beef stock and bring to full simmer, until sauce thickens. Add in corn and peas, and heat through, about 1 minute.

Spoon mixture into a prepared, 10-inch round baking dish or a square pan. If serving a crowd, this recipe doubles well and fits nicely in a 9x13 inch pan. Spread the mashed potato topping evenly over the beef mixture.

This is the point where you stop and pack up the meal. Cover the dish, place it into a sturdy box and deliver with your blessings.

INSTRUCTIONS FOR RECIPIENT

Before serving, the recipient should bake at 350 degree F until the filling is hot, the topping is lightly browned, and the edges are bubbly and just beginning to get crispy, about 35 minutes. Remove from the oven and sprinkle with 1 cup cheddar cheese. Return to the oven and bake for 10 minutes more. Remove from the oven. Let rest for 10 minutes. Sprinkle 2 tablespoons fresh-chopped parsley to garnish before serving.

WINTER

i wake suddenly

… and lie still, listening for what I thought had awakened me. Yes, there it is — a frenzied yipping. Flinging off the covers and swinging still sleepy legs over the edge of the bed, a chill runs the length of my body as my bare feet touch the rough wood floor. Fumbling in the dark for my robe, the lonely howl comes again, closer this time, making my heart pump wildly. Down the creaky old stairs I stumble, slinging on my muck boots and my winter wrap as I head out into the cold night. The moon is bright as it lights my path, and a frost has settled, glistening in the snow.

Ahead is the warm glow given off by the heat lamp left on during chilly winter nights to keep the ladies of the coop comfy. My eyes begin frantically searching for signs of life while my heart beats out its crazy rhythm; a wave of relief then washes over me. Yes, yes, I did close the door.

There are many times I doubt my memory to keep up with the daily tasks of the farm. I peer in, all the hens nestled together warm, and, in a row, I count softly under my breath, one, two, three, four … all 35 accounted for. They coo and cluck sleepily as if to tell me that all is calm. In this moment, I agree.

The night sky is clear as I make my way back toward the house. Stopping for a moment to admire the stars, my father's voice is carried on the wind, and brings me back to when I was little, when he said: "And that is Orion's Belt, and look off there, my dear. That is the Big Dipper. See how it bends?" Now, with childlike wonder, I gaze up into the vast inky blackness, pin pricked with points of light and am filled with awe once again.

The house is warm. I stir the glowing embers in the wood stove and toss in a few more pieces, rubbing my hands together and holding them closer as it starts to crackle and pop.

The old grandfather clock chimes four times, low and steady. Though my body longs for more sleep, my mind is awake and ready to start the day. I shuffle my way into the kitchen, flick on the soft light over the old stove, and set about with the morning routine. Dark coffee begins perking, thick slabs of bacon sizzle, and with renewed gratitude, farm-fresh eggs are cracked and whisked into a fluffy omelet.

There will be much to accomplish on this day and the days to follow in the lead-up to the holidays. But in these quiet moments, I am grateful for the hubbub and preparation that lays ahead. It is planned chaos, unlike the kind brought on if there had been a coyote in the hen house!

BETH

wayne

To everything there is a season, and a time to every purpose
under the heavens.
                                        Ecclesiastes 3:1

As with the seasons of the garden, there is a circle of life.
In spring, tiny seeds are tucked beneath the warming earth to
germinate and shoot up into tender green periscopes, expanding
and flourishing, bringing brilliant color to the garden and hope
to the gardener. The flower beds and vegetable patches become a
sweep of texture and bloom proclaiming, "I am here, I am here!"

Each year, I am delighted by the splendor of this vibrant show,
proud of my labor of love, and grateful for the bounty and
beauty the earth offers up. Spring surrenders to summer. The
days grow long and hot with no clouds or rain in sight. This
daily stress takes its toll, sucking out life, cracking the soil and
bringing the garden to her knees no matter how hard I try to
keep her fed. Fall finds shades of honey-brown taking the place
where once verdant colors played.

There are waves of dried wheat, grasses, and brittle pods dancing
in the wind like a rolling ocean, a resplendent maturity that
marks the season of the golden age. The seed heads, skeletons of
once majestic blooms, will live on into the winter, sustaining life,

feeding all creatures both winged and furry. As the cool winds
and rains of fall bring relief to the parched ground, plants cease
to put forth energy, leaving the last bloom exposed atop the
stem, its depleted petals like fine parchment paper, feather soft
and hauntingly sweet. It finally surrenders as the winter takes her
with first frost. She is covered tenderly with a glistening blanket
and gently laid to rest.

> Like a Victorian-era envelope edged in black,
> a text message stops me in my tracks with a few
> words: Wayne has passed away.

A primal sob, a wave of relief that his suffering has ended, and
he has moved on to a land beyond pain, a place of rest. And yet
a chasm is slashed through my heart; deep, dark, and agonizing.
We gather, talking late into the night of his amazing love for us,
his silly side and stubborn streak, our emotions veering wildly.

The days that follow run together. I look out at the world
as it continues to turn and feel as if I'm frozen, unable to
comprehend this ending. I am standing still, and hollow. Today,
I do the only thing I can to help ease my pain and give comfort
to my sister. I cook a hearty meal of soup, add some bread, and
include a few fresh baked cookies. I tuck these into a basket with
a bottle of wine.

As I arrive at her home, rain is pouring and the wind has kicked
up. I am reminded of the last words Wayne spoke to our younger

sister when she stopped in that morning for a hug and to show him some stones she had collected on her trail run:
"I'm waiting on the rains," he said in his quiet manner.

The kitchen is warm as I enter. A candle burns bright, flicking shadows on the wall; old-school country tunes play softly and hushed voices from those gathered in the living room reminisce about a great father, husband, and son.

Long hugs greet me as we settle in to chat over the funeral plans; so much care and detail given for someone deeply loved. I make notes, trying to focus, while it takes all my efforts to hold back the tears that are raging in the vast hole left in my soul.

His black cowboy hat rides shotgun as I make my way home. Unburdening myself to this silent partner, I can no longer hold the pain in place. Emotions of gratitude flood my heart at the honor I feel to create flowers for someone so loved; a man who lived in a way that was honest and real.

The setting sun casts a ray of light through the rain, a watery beam glistening over the misty rolling hills, and a peace enters my being. I am no stranger to change or seasons. The garden teaches me this each year.

It is winter now, but spring will come again.

BETH

seasonal rituals

These days, I take our two children to the woods to gather fresh evergreens to bedeck our house. Christmas is just around the corner, and I'm feeling the pull of the world to keep up with its glitz and gluttony. My mind wants to slow it down and keep life simpler, enjoying these little moments and holding the children close, as I know they will only be young for a short while.

The need to impart these simple rituals of the season is paramount in my heart and mind. The joy I seek is often felt tromping through the natural world, and I cherish creating holiday memories that center around nature, rather than at a shopping mall or with the arrival of the delivery truck.

> With such a Norman Rockwell childhood comes the challenge of living up to its standard.

Yes, I realize I am remembering with my child's brain, but the hurdle one makes into present-day reality is sometimes daunting. The kiddos this morning would have been more than happy to remain in rumpled pajamas until well past noon, devouring bowls of Panda Puff cereal and watching Saturday morning cartoons. Instead, they grumble, pull on boots and jackets, and load into the back seat of the car, immediately starting to bicker

over whose turn it was to pick the music.

Bumping along the muddy-rutted firebreak that runs between fields, and down the twisting road that leads to the canyon, I am beginning to doubt that this was a rational decision. Suddenly, somewhere between the tinny voices of Alvin and Theodore's rendition of "We've been good, but we can't wait; please Christmas, don't be late," and Bing Crosby's crooning, the mood shifts and settles. Eyes move to the pine trees towering over us like so many turrets of a mythical green castle, and the dense rough trunks become secret passageways leading from one land to the next.

They spring out of the car, and little booted feet hit the ground. They listen for the voices of woodland fairies; they look in the dark shadows for elfin kings, and inhale the scent of rain-drenched bark and pine. The crisp winter air is whistling about, ruffling their hair, reddening their soft cheeks.

I grab my gardening clippers and canvas bag and set to work, using my fingernails to scrape moss off the north side of a tree, and my clippers to snip low-hanging boughs. Bare twigs and spongy mushrooms are foraged and assembled in wicker baskets. They will be transformed into miniature woodland villages, wreaths, mantel decor, and cushions for delicate vintage baubles and bits.

When all is loaded in the back of the car, I call the kids, who are now whooping wildly and running like deer through the underbrush in hot pursuit of some magical but elusive creature.

I must admire the fort made of spruce branches, then play a game of Pooh-sticks on the bridge spanning the overflowing Pudding River, and hoist myself over the metal gate, now slick with a thin sheen of ice, to view the cows bedded down among the trees in the far meadow.

They are satisfied at last. We hike back to the car, and I drive in the direction of home. Their heads are full of adventures, imagined and real; while fingers are thawing, thanks to the blasting heater, the tunes of Sarah McLachlan wrap us in a blanket of serenity.

There's a pile of muddy coats and galoshes by the back door and the children have left a trail of wet footprints from the bathtub to their bedrooms. Broccoli crowns on the counter wait to be transformed into a savory soup. But first, I pop slices of white bread into the toaster. I scoop cocoa and sugar into a saucepan and pour milk into a Pyrex measuring cup.

Whisking cinnamon and sugar together, I liberally sprinkle crispy wedges with the sweet concoction, before piling it all on a plate. I pour the hot chocolate into mugs and top with marshmallow whip. Following voices, I find them in the living room, surrounded by books: *Wind in the Willows, A Door in the Wall, A Time to Keep, The Sleepy Dormouse,* and *The Night Before Christmas.*

As I make my way back towards the kitchen, I hear excited, but hushed tones as the children whisper secrets of gifts made in art class and wishes of presents from Santa. I smile, knowing that snapshots in my head may be drastically different from theirs, but the feelings of comfort and joy must be the same.

SARAH

cinnamon sugar toast

SERVES: 2

In our family, our mama's Cinnamon Sugar Toast has been the comfort food of choice for all of us. The toast is the answer for long days in wild wind chasing wayward calves or the heartbreak of missing the school bus. It is a culinary answer to stress, like a little kid's favorite blanket, warm and soothing, but with a few crunchy spots.

PREP TIME: 5 minutes

COOK TIME: 11-12 minutes

INGREDIENTS

4 slices of white bread (homemade bread or thick-sliced brioche)

¼ cup softened salted butter

¼ cup granulated sugar

1 teaspoon ground cinnamon

½ teaspoon vanilla extract

INSTRUCTIONS

In a medium bowl, combine softened butter, sugar, cinnamon, and vanilla. Stir with a fork until the mixture forms a uniform paste. Divide the mixture evenly among the slices of bread; spread from edge to edge, covering slices completely.

Place pieces of bread on a broiler-safe, ungreased, and unlined baking sheet. Place the baking sheet on the center rack of oven, at least 5 inches from the broiler. Broil for 10-12 minutes until the edges of the bread are golden brown and the cinnamon-sugar is bubbling.

If at any time the edges begin to burn, pull the baking sheet out of the oven. Watch closely! Do not wander away during this stage.

Cut toast into triangles and serve with hot chocolate.

come as you are

Have I mentioned I adore entertaining? Usually, the mood strikes me at say, seven o'clock on a Friday evening as the weekend looms large and lush before me, and a glass of red wine is warming my inners. The craving of companionship and need for new voices drive me to tap out an invitation into my phone.

Are you free tomorrow? Come as you are! No, no, bring nothing but your fabulous self and your sidekick. Absolutely can't wait! *Ta-ta xoxo.*

Saturday. I'm in spin class. My head is a jumble of recipes as it tries to sort a list of groceries while keeping up with the overly caffeinated and energetic instructor shouting orders to up the resistance and push to the top of our imaginary hill.

Sweaty and rumpled, I take that momentum to the aisles of our local grocery store, careening around corners and charging down open spaces. I weave in and out of the dawdling, lazy, weekend shoppers.

Home again, home again, jiggety-jog. I dump groceries on the kitchen counter, perishables are shoved into the refrigerator, while the rest are left where they lie. I scrub my hands and tie an apron around my yoga tights. From the cupboards, I take out sugar and flour. There's a flurry of creaming as the mixer twerks itself across the counter.

There's harissa sauce to be assembled and rubbed into every nook and cranny of the boneless pork shoulder, broccolini to be washed along with the kale and a large bunch of bright chard that has been plucked from the winter garden. A garlicky hazelnut and lemon concoction ready to chop, zest, and mix, and a baguette of sourdough to be slathered with a blend of anchovies and roasted garlic that has been simmering in olive oil and unsalted butter.

I used to go over-the-top with hors d'oeuvres, but have found some roasted nuts and a wedge of cheese is an uncomplicated way to start the evening. Nobody wants to begin the night with dribbles down her dress from fancy ensembles that require the balancing of small plates and fussy bites.

Then, there is always a moment where the question "What was I thinking?" screams into my thoughts. Usually, it's about an hour before the guests arrive and there are still dishes in the sink, and no flowers on the table.

I've been known to stack pots and pans on the washing machine and fill the laundry room counter with caked-on spatulas and spoons to be attacked once the evening is over.

If I were a planner, the table would be set the night before and a lovely arrangement assembled the previous day. Since I'm usually not that organized, I've found that individual flowers in petite vases do quite nicely and when nothing else is blooming, a few evergreen sprigs will give you that festive look.

Dim the lights, select a jazzy or mellow playlist, slick on some bright red lipstick, and pour yourself a short glass of chilled Pinot Gris. Breathe. Nobody likes to feel as if they are a burden, which defeats the purpose of having loved ones over. They will (as we all do) be honored to see your real side, rather than the one we show the world day-to-day. Let them in, truly let them in, regardless of whether dinner is served on time, or if the meat is overdone, and the side dishes are at room temperature (this is the reason to meet everyone at the door with a glass of champagne). Everyone will go away feeling cherished and cocooned by the embrace of warm and honest friendship.

SARAH'S GO-TO MENU FOR WINTER GATHERINGS

Pre-dinner snacks

Provençal-style roasted nuts, a wedge of something like a Stilton or an earthy, triple-cream Jersey cows' milk cheese

Champagne

An assortment of red wines and a chilled white or two

Harissa-Rubbed Pork Shoulder with White Beans and Chard

Garlicky Broccolini and Kale Greens with Hazelnuts and Coriander

Caramelized Garlic on Toasted Sourdough with Anchovies

Celery and Fennel with Toasted Walnuts and Blue Cheese

I like to serve the celery and fennel salad, or any salad, after the main course. Think of it as a palate cleanser.

Dessert can be anything easy, a favorite is tiny, salty, chocolate-y cookies, freshly baked and tantalizingly soft, made from dough previously prepared and stored in the freezer.

Even simpler, I purchase fancy Maraschino cherries, and offer them in a ramekin for mindless nibbling. They keep the party from taking itself too seriously, as we sip dark coffee or a smooth Scotch and solve the world's problems.

Stay at the table. Enjoy being present in the moment with a full belly and the best of friends. The dishes can wait until the last goodbye hug has been squeezed out, and tail lights are distant red dots.

SARAH

harissa-rubbed pork shoulder

SERVES: 6-8

Adapted with permission from the cookbook, Nothing Fancy
*by Alison Roman, this recipe is the queen of dinner party
tables in all seasons. It calls for an affordable cut of meat, and is
almost impossible to get wrong. Its flavors are fabulous!*

PREP TIME: 25 minutes

COOK TIME: 4 hours 15 minutes

PREHEAT oven to 325 degrees F

INGREDIENTS

4 lbs. boneless pork shoulder, rubbed with kosher salt and fresh ground pepper

½ cup harissa paste

¼ cup distilled white vinegar

3 tablespoons tomato paste

3 tablespoons light brown sugar

4 garlic cloves, finely grated

1 ½ cups water

2 (15-ounce) cans small white beans, such as cannellini or great northern, drained and rinsed.

1 bunch chard, stems removed, leaves torn into bite-sized pieces

1 cup cilantro, tender leaves and stems

1 lemon, halved

INSTRUCTIONS

Season the pork with salt and pepper.

Combine the harissa paste, vinegar, tomato paste, brown sugar, and garlic in a medium bowl. Smear the mixture over the pork roast and its nooks and crannies. Place in a large Dutch oven, add the water and place the lid on the pot. Roast until the pork is nearly falling-apart tender, 3 to 3 ½ hours.

Remove from the oven, add the beans, and season with additional salt and pepper. Increase the oven temperature to 425 degrees F. and return the pot to the oven, uncovered. Roast until the beans have soaked up all the liquid and the top of the pork is deep golden brown, approximately 40-45 minutes.

Transfer the pork to a cutting board. Slice pork into ½-inch slices (if it shreds, that's fine). Add the chard to the beans and stir to wilt the leaves. Transfer beans and greens to a large serving platter or iron skillet and place pork on top.

the magic of the season

It was special for us growing up; it was a time of warmth, laughter, and the joy of being together as family. Our parents were rich in life but not in material things. They worked with what they had, and in doing so, created pure magic for us.

Tradition was strong in our upbringing. When it was time to pick the tree, our annual selection had to fall under the strict criteria of past years. The tree must be the biggest, the most perfect in the field; it mustn't have holes and its branches needed to be strong enough to be fully loaded with our decorations. The van was packed with rosy-cheeked, bundled-up children all singing in chorus as our mother and father led us in song, "Oh, Holy Night, the stars are brightly shining … ." We continued in rambling harmony, lifting our voices, perhaps not singing the exact lyrics, but doing it wholeheartedly.

At the tree farm in the Silverton Hills of Oregon, we clambered out, one by one, and the search was on. Back home, the tree that appeared so small in the ground could barely fit through our front door. The top had to be cut, then, the bottom. This process would start with much merriment as Dad yanked on the chainsaw and black smoke and fumes belched back at us. We would all jostle for positions to hold the trunk still, our faces buried deep in the soft, sweetly-scented pine needles. A few more adjustments, and then, with a great heave-ho, through the door the tree popped, accompanied with the lot of us toppling in after it. Our mother, standing in the kitchen doorway with a

baby on her hip, and smiling at us all, would kindly chide, "Give your father room, girls," and we would drop back a few inches. Undeterred, Dad worked with gusto to ensure the tree appeared elegantly straight, with the assistance of a few old magazines and a book or two strategically wedged beneath the tree stand.

The mechanics of this installation completed, Mom came in bearing tin TV trays laden with piles of golden-brown toast triangles, slathered with butter, topped with cinnamon sugar, and which had been placed under the broiler. The result was a delicate caramelized crunch on top, and a soft, slightly gooey underside. Accompanying these treats were steaming mugs of rich chocolate milk made from the recipe on the back of the cocoa tin, topped with a handful of melting mini marshmallows. We munched happily, gazing at the naked tree before us, knowing if this year would be like the previous ones, a whole slew of giddy days lay ahead.

Tomorrow, tree decorating; first, the lights, including our '70s bulbs in matte gold, burnt orange, and avocado green, followed by percolating bubble lights, and the string of crusted globes and random chipped stars. Then we adorned the tree with our eclectic assortment of ornaments, most of the arts-and-crafts variety, done in one classroom or another and usually involving traced hands made into snowmen, or wise men, or something indistinguishable, but covered in oodles of glitter and made with the utmost amount love.

Dad would then hang one strand of tinsel at a time until each branch glittered like a 1930s showgirl. The crowning of the tree: the gaudy star of Bethlehem as it shone with multi-colored lights and a number of settings ranging from disco to a mellow-groovy-mood vibe. Last (and done with reverence), was the Christmas bell, a deep blue beauty that housed a music box inside; its tinkling melody signaled the holiday had truly begun.

Each year was the camp-out under the Christmas tree, our heads forming a semi-circle under its lights, as we drifted off to sleep with the scent of pine. There was an almost uncontrollable level of excitement as we waited for grandma's yearly gift check. If it was delayed by the busy postal season, it would postpone the present-buying, with some years seeing our parents scampering out as late as Christmas Eve!

Mom and Dad would work until the wee hours, wrapping each gift with care and attaching a festive well-used bow with masking tape for extra flair. Morning would find them rising early to plug in the tree lights, putting the Vienna Boy's Choir on the stereo, and, after a much-deserved pot of coffee was perked, allowing the lot of us to tumble down the stairs where we had gathered en masse.

They watched with delighted smiles as we stood in awe before the tree, taking in its neatly organized gifts and our stockings bulging in their thumb-tacked row along the bookshelf. There was a fire in the wood stove, and warm Christmas tree bread studded with candied fruit, citrus rind, and golden raisins, all smothered in an almond sugar glaze awaited us.

We would sit crisscross-applesauce on the floor, or claim our section of the sofa, as gifts were handed out. Each one of us took a turn, basking in the oohs and aahs of the others as paper fell away to reveal the treasure inside.

Unbeknownst to us at the time, the greatest gift we were given during those years was that of family, the example of self-sacrifice for the good of others, and an enduring love and commitment to all who inhabited the space within those walls.

BETH & SARAH

old fashioned hot cocoa

SERVES: 4

When the outside world looks like a Currier and Ives winter postcard, numb fingers and cold rosy noses require some help. Give a shivering loved one a steaming cup of cocoa and suddenly all is glowing once again! Spice up this rich cocoa for grownups with a splash of peppermint Schnapps for an added little spark — and clink mugs with friends all around.

PREP TIME: 5 minutes

COOK TIME: 8-10 minutes

INGREDIENTS

¾ cup white sugar

⅓ cup unsweetened cocoa

⅓ cup boiling water

3½ cups milk

¾ teaspoon vanilla extract

½ cup half-and-half

INSTRUCTIONS

Combine sugar, cocoa powder, and salt in a saucepan. Add boiling water and whisk until smooth. Bring mixture to a simmer and cook for 2 minutes. Stir constantly to prevent scorching.

Stir in 3-½ cups of milk and heat until very hot, but do not boil. Remove from heat; add vanilla.

Divide cocoa among 4 mugs. Add half-and-half to each mug in order to cool cocoa to drinking temperature.

Add whipping cream and orange zest if desired.

betweenmas

That yawning week connecting Christmas and New Year's Day is full of overindulgences in every category. The sleeping in past seven, lazily luxuriating in a nest created by a heavy duvet and crisp cotton sheets. We savor slow starts to the day, while camped out on the sofa with cups of strong-brewed dark Colombian coffee. Picking apart a warmed croissant, its crumbs gather on the front of my silk pajamas, I relish the thought of an open-ended day stretching before me.

Morning melts into afternoon with everyone pondering what to do. Some ambitious guests head out to trek the trails at Silver Falls Park, while others opt for mimosa and jazz tunes while preparing quiche and fruit salad for the returning adventurers.

Evening settles her arms around us as champagne bubbles in coupe glasses. Stew simmers gently on the stove. Rolls are baking, and crispy green lettuce leaves are tossed with a bright vinaigrette. Red wine is poured, and dinner is served. Lengthy conversation, low lights, soft music, and the glow from candles slide us slowly into the night.

That's how it would be in a perfect world. Reality? It's lying in bed, sheets tangled, mouths cottony from too much wine and not enough sleep. It's missed gym workouts due to the stacks of cars in the driveway, and the jitters from excessive caffeine. Meals are a hodgepodge and disorganized, a collision of collective efforts as timetables are in constant flux. Clean towels are scarce, hot water is short, as are quiet moments or personal sanity.

Betweenmas is a blend of the real and idealized, leading us to exhale in relief when we can resume our normal routines.

We lug out the needle-dropping tree and scrape the remaining double dark chocolate cookie bars into the garbage to avoid temptation. Christmas baubles and bits are stored in the basement once again as are the sleeping bags and air mattresses that were provided for out-of-town guests.

Now, the post-holiday nesting can begin! Fire is essential. To our primal selves, it speaks of home, safety, and comfort. Be it a blaze in the hearth or a glow of candlelight, we are drawn like moths to the flame. In the enticing, hypnotizing, soothing warmth of the flame's companionship, our anxieties, striving, and busy-ness fade.

The hope of spring is suggested by bulbs nestled in terra-cotta pots or antique dishes that have been filled with gravel or moss. Coaxed to send up vibrant shoots of glossy green, we will soon see a kaleidoscope of color and be able to inhale the sweet perfume of hyacinth, narcissus, and delicately scented lily-of-the-valley.

A fresh start in a cozy, clutter-free environment is an invitation to re-evaluate what is important in the coming year with a clear mind and hopeful heart. Truly, I find this post-holiday season one of my favorite times, as it feels like anything is possible, and the world is a blank page.

SARAH

ome

Life growing up in a big family had its twists and turns, like most families we suppose. But in ours, the level of everything was magnified twelvefold. There were children gleefully playing or arguing, babies crying, toddlers and teens whining, and endless dishes and mountains of laundry were the order of the day.

We don't know how our mother stayed intact. But we think she managed by focusing on what was in front of her in the moment, what needs had to be met, or what required her full attention.

She woke before the rest of the house did, brewed fresh coffee, exchanged a few words with our father, who kissed her on the cheek and went off to work. She stood on the porch waving goodbye until he was out of sight.

Before she set about her work for the morning, she found time to enjoy the quiet with coffee and the Good Book, or she hummed a hymn preparing her heart for the day to come. These were the essential keys to holding it all together.

Both of our parents found pure joy in the simple life they created and even though it wasn't always perfect, it was a life formed out of a pure love, at the heart of which were their twelve children.

The path they took wasn't easy, but they started on it too young to know any better or wiser. They forged ahead together, pursuing a life of joy, and shaping their children into who we are today.

What do we take away from the memories that are stored in our gray matter? We reached out to all our siblings, and though varied in tone and shaped by the space and experiences since each of us flew the nest, the answers all contained one word: Home. We have a shared joy in using what is available, confidence in creating, if not a masterpiece, then at least something assembled with love.

In honoring the effort put forth on our behalf as children, we strive to do the same for our own broods by encouraging creativity, individuality, and a good work ethic. Old-fashioned ideas are rearranged and updated to serve the same purpose they did for us, our parents, and grandparents.

We hope, as all humans do, to leave this place a little kinder and a little greener. And above all else, to create an abundance of bonding events for the next generation that will help shape their own sense of home.

BETH & SARAH